CW00552883

M

The Church of Jesus Christ
of Latter-day Saints

A Catholic Perspective

by
Jimmy Akin

All booklets are published thanks to the
generous support of the members of the
Catholic Truth Society

CATHOLIC TRUTH SOCIETY
PUBLISHERS TO THE HOLY SEE

Contents

Basic Questions about Mormonism

What is Mormonism?

Mormonism is a religion that started in the United States in the 1800s. It was founded by Joseph Smith, Jr., who lived near Palmyra, New York. He reported visions of God the Father, Jesus Christ, and angels. Mormons believe that under the guidance of an angel he found a set of Golden Plates from which he translated The Book of Mormon. Those who adhered to this book became known as "Mormons."

After the publication of the book, Joseph Smith founded a church, which was initially called the Church of Christ. It was not related to other churches with the same name. This church grew and changed names several times. Its headquarters also was relocated several times, to places in Ohio, Missouri, and Illinois. After Joseph Smith's death, a succession crisis occurred in its leadership, causing the movement to fragment.

One of the resulting groups migrated to what is now the state of Utah, under the leadership of a man named Brigham Young, who established a new headquarters in Salt Lake City. This church today is formally known as The Church of Jesus Christ of Latter-day Saints and it is the largest of the Mormon offshoots. In 2005 it had twelve and a half million members worldwide, about half of whom are in the United States. The other offshoots of the original church are much smaller. The total number of individuals claiming to follow Joseph Smith may be about thirteen million. Because of the prominence of the Salt Lake City church in Mormonism, this booklet will focus primarily on it.

Members of this church often prefer to be called "Latter-day Saints" or simply "Saints," though the term "Mormon" is in general use in America.

What do Mormons believe?

Mormons reject the doctrines of traditional Christianity. According to Joseph Smith, who is regarded as a prophet, the early Church departed from the faith taught by Jesus Christ in an event known as "the Great Apostasy." He was thus led to form his own church to introduce "restored Christianity" into the world.

The teachings that Smith imparted to his followers evolved over time and continued to evolve after his death. Today the Mormon church teaches a set of doctrines that traditional Christians often find shocking.

At the core of Mormon teaching is the claim that there is more than one god, meaning that Mormons are polytheists. They hold that there is a race of divine beings that serve as the gods of different worlds. These gods are male or female and propagate by sexual reproduction. Furthermore, mankind is part of this species, and it is possible for a man to become a god with his own world to govern.

Mormons also hold that we, as individuals, were not created by God. Instead, we existed from all eternity as intelligences. At some point these intelligences were born as "spirit children" to God the Father and his wife (or one of his wives; some Mormon sources indicate that God is polygamous). To further our development, we were then born into this world as the children of our earthly parents.

This path, Mormons believe, was followed by God the Father himself, who began as an eternal intelligence and then took on spirit and flesh and eventually progressed to his current, glorified state. By following in his footsteps, we too can become gods, equal to where the Father is now, though technically he will always be ahead of us since he, too, is eternally progressing to greater degrees of glory.

What works do Mormons honour as scripture?

Mormons honour the Holy Bible as the word of God "as far as it is translated correctly" (*Articles of Faith* 8). The latter clause is important since it allows Mormons to assert that when Scripture appears to contradict their doctrines, it is an instance when Scripture has been mistranslated.

Mormons accept the Protestant canon of Scripture, which means that they do not accept the seven deuterocanonical books found in the Catholic Old Testament. When dealing with outsiders, Mormons generally use the King James Version of the Bible. Among themselves they occasionally use a version of the King James Bible that was altered by Joseph Smith to correct alleged mistranslations in it and bring it into conformity with Mormon doctrine.

In addition to the Bible, Mormons also honour several other works as scripture. The most famous of these is the Book of Mormon, from which the name "Mormon" derives. This work is sometimes referred to as "Another Testament of Jesus Christ" and purports to give the history of ancient Hebrew immigrants to the Americas and Jesus' appearance to them after his ministry in the Holy Land.

The third work that Mormons regard as scripture is a book known as Doctrine and Covenants, which consists of revelations reportedly given to Joseph Smith and other Mormon leaders.

The final work of Mormon scripture is known as The Pearl of Great Price. This contains several shorter works, including portions of Joseph Smith's revisions of Genesis and Matthew. It also contains a short, autobiographical statement by Joseph Smith and a document known as the Book of Abraham. Finally, it includes a brief statement of thirteen Articles of Faith.

What sacraments does the Mormon church have?

The Mormon church does not use the term "sacraments." Instead, it prefers the term "ordinances." There are a variety of ordinances that are practiced in Mormonism.

The most important ordinances are those considered necessary for achieving godhood. These are referred to as "saving ordinances." They include baptism and confirmation. For men, ordination to what are known as the "Aaronic" and "Melchizedek" priesthoods is also required. There are also two ordinances practiced only in Mormon temples that fall into this class. They are known as the "temple endowment" and the "sealing" of marriages.

In addition, there are a variety of lesser ordinances that are not considered necessary for godhood. These include the naming and blessing of children, consecration of oils, graves, and church buildings, and the Mormon equivalents of the Eucharist and the anointing of the sick. These latter two are respectively referred to as "the Sacrament" and "administering to the sick and afflicted."

Though some of these ordinances have recognisably Christian roots, they are often understood or applied in markedly different ways. For example, baptism is only given to children after they reach the age of accountability (equivalent to the age of reason), which in Mormonism is deemed to be about eight years of age (Catholicism regards it as generally about seven). Infant baptism is expressly rejected. Similarly, "the Sacrament" is not believed to be the Body and Blood of Christ, but only a symbolic reminder of Christ. Belief in the Real Presence is expressly rejected, the ceremony for the Sacrament is minimal, and it is typically celebrated with store-bought bread and with water instead of wine.

How do Mormons worship?

On a typical Sunday, Mormons spend three hours at services at a local meeting house or chapel. These services fall into three parts, though the order of the parts may vary.

One part, which lasts a little more than an hour, involves the entire congregation and is known as a Sacrament Meeting. This is a non-liturgical service that involves the distribution of the Mormon equivalent of Holy Communion. It also involves hymns, prayers, lay sermons, and testimonials.

In another part of the services, the congregation is then divided into groups. Very young children are placed in a nursery, and children between four and twelve are placed in a Sunday school known as "Primary," where they will remain for the rest of the morning. Older children and adults are divided into groups to attend other Sunday school classes, but they do not last for the rest of the morning.

For the remaining part of the services, the congregation is divided by gender. Men and boys older than twelve have a short meeting for prayer, a hymn, and announcements and then divide into groups according to the level of priesthood they have received, which tends to follow along with their age. Meanwhile, the women and girls older than twelve have a similar joint meeting before dividing into groups by age.

In addition to Sunday services, there are many other meetings held at Mormon chapels throughout the week, except on Monday night, which is reserved for an event known as "Family Home Evening" - a home-based event involving singing, prayer, scripture reading, lessons, and activities.

What are Mormon temples?

Temples are special buildings that Mormons also use for worship. There are over a hundred temples at different places in the world (mostly in North America). Unlike local chapels, temples are not open to the public and, in fact, they are not open to many Mormons. An individual church member must be deemed "temple worthy" and receive an official "temple recommend" in order to participate at the services at such a site.

There are a number of special ceremonies that are performed in temples. These include the ordinances known as the "endowment," which is viewed as a bestowal of "power from on high" and is one of the ordinances necessary for a Mormon to achieve godhood.

Additionally, believers may participate in another ordinance known as "sealing." This ordinance is thought to make family relationships (between husband and wife or between parents and children) permanent so that it will be possible for individuals to remain a family in the afterlife.

Besides the endowment and sealings that individuals perform for themselves in temples there are also a great number of ordinances performed by proxy on behalf of the dead. These include proxy baptisms, confirmations, priesthood ordinations, endowments, and sealings. It is held that these proxy ordinances will make it possible for the deceased who never heard or embraced the Mormon gospel to be able to achieve godhood in the afterlife, should they choose to receive the benefits of these ordinances.

Mormons are very secretive about these rites, stating that they are sacred. They will often refuse to discuss them or discuss them in detail. Former Mormons, however, have revealed their contents, and transcripts of what is said and done in them are available on the Internet.

Many non-Mormon groups have found the idea of Mormons performing proxy baptisms, marriages, and other ordinances for their departed loved ones or church leaders (e.g., former popes) to be extremely offensive and lodge strong objections against this practice.

What must a Mormon do to attend a temple?

To obtain a temple recommend, Mormons must meet a variety of requirements, including having one or more interviews to establish that they are temple worthy. Such interviews cover matters such as their belief in Mormon doctrine and their practice of Mormon morals. Among other things, the latter involves observing what are known as the "Law of Chastity" (not having sexual relations with someone to whom one is not married) and the "Word of Wisdom."

The Word of Wisdom is a revelation Joseph Smith claimed to have received concerning the proper way to live (*Doctrine and Covenants 89*). It was originally given as a matter of advice rather than obligation, though this was later changed. The Word of Wisdom advises against the use of tobacco, wine and strong drinks, and "hot drinks" (now interpreted as meaning those with caffeine). It also counselled against eating meat except in the winter time, but this part of the Word of Wisdom is not treated as obligatory. Under the terms of the original Word of Wisdom, beer - as a "mild drink" - was allowed, but it has subsequently been prohibited.

How is the Mormon church organised?

The organisational system of the Mormon church is complex. In the ideal, an individual congregation is known as a "ward" and is presided over by a bishop.

Three to sixteen neighbouring wards are then organised
into a larger unit known as a "stake," which is presided
over by the "stake president." In some cases, though,
there are circumstances (such as not enough members)
that prevent the organisation of wards and stakes, in
which case their equivalent bodies are respectively known
as "branches" and "districts."

If the ward and the stake are the basic units of
organisation at the lowest level of the Mormon church,
the Quorum of the Twelve Apostles and the First
Presidency represent its highest.

The Quorum of the Twelve Apostles consists of twelve
men who are considered fully equivalent to biblical
apostles. Above them is the First Presidency, a group
typically made up of three men, each of whom has the
title "President."

One of these, however, is superior to the other two and
is regarded as the highest leader of the church, with the
other two serving as his counsellors. This man has an
office equivalent to that of Joseph Smith, Jr. and is
regarded as his successor, being the "prophet, seer, and
revelator" of the church. Upon the death of the prophet,
the most senior apostle is chosen to replace him.

The other two members of the First Presidency are
typically apostles as well, and between the First
Presidency and the Quorum of the Twelve the Mormon
church typically claims a total of fifteen apostles.

Between its lowest and highest levels of organisation, the Mormon church also has a variety of intermediate structures and organisations, as well as ministries involving particular groups, such as women and children.

What Mormon splinter groups are there?

There have been a considerable number of Mormon splinter groups, most of which are very small. Some were founded in the succession crisis that occurred after the death of Joseph Smith in 1844. While Brigham Young was eventually established as the leader of the majority of Mormons, others attached themselves to other Mormon leaders, resulting in different offshoots.

The largest of the offshoots was founded in 1860 by Joseph Smith III, the eldest son of Joseph Smith, Jr. For much of its history it was known as the Reorganised Church of Jesus Christ of Latter Day Saints (RLDS), but in 2001 it changed its name to the Community of Christ. It shares many Mormon distinctives, including belief in the Book of Mormon and an edition of Doctrine and Covenants as scripture, but it also has important doctrinal differences. Most notably, it does not believe in the existence of multiple gods. Its view of the godhead has undergone development in recent years and today recognises one God in three Persons, though at times it uses language that makes it sound as if the Father, the Son, and the Spirit might be different modes in which

God exists rather than distinct Persons. The Community of Christ is the largest Mormon offshoot, and it reports about a quarter of a million members in fifty countries.

While the Community of Christ is the largest offshoot, the attention of the American press is more often drawn to a much smaller group of offshoots who are collectively referred to as "fundamentalist Mormons." These groups continue to hold to doctrines and practices that over time have been cast off by the main Mormon church, including the practice of polygamy and the exclusion of black people from the Mormon priesthood. There are a few tens of thousands of such Mormons, and they attract notable attention by the press because their practice of polygamy is illegal and because some of them permit illegal marriages with underage girls. These groups are strongly disapproved of by the main Mormon church.

Is Mormonism Christian?

One must be validly baptised in order to be a Christian. Baptism is the first sacrament of Christian initiation, by which one becomes a member of Christ (cf. *CCC* 1212-1213). Whether Mormons are Christians thus depends on whether they have a valid baptism.

This matter was clarified in a response by the Congregation for the Doctrine of the Faith dated 5th June, 2001. The response, signed by then-Cardinal Joseph Ratzinger (later Pope Benedict XVI) and approved by

Pope John Paul II, considered the question of whether the baptism administered by The Church of Jesus Christ of Latter-day Saints is valid, and the reply was negative.

Lacking a valid baptism, Mormonism cannot be regarded as Christian. Its theology also involves a radically different vision of God and man than that proclaimed by the Christian faith.

None of this is to attribute personal fault to Mormons, who may be sincere individuals practicing their religion in good conscience. It is simply a recognition that, objectively speaking, Mormonism is not Christian since it lacks the doctrinal and sacramental foundations of the Christian faith.

What relations do Mormons have with Christians?

Mormonism originally had a very antagonistic relationship with Christians as Joseph Smith claimed that all of the churches of his day were corrupt, requiring him to start a new one.

Verbal attacks on Christian groups were common in Mormon literature, and the Catholic Church was singled out with special hostility. The Book of Mormon refers to a "great and abominable church" which is founded by the devil and which was worse than all other churches (1 *Nephi* 13). This church is described in terms that are strongly suggestive of the Catholic Church, as it was portrayed in 19th century anti-Catholic polemics, and later Mormons did not hesitate to identify it as such.

Mormons, for their part, were viewed with hostility by ordinary Christian groups, who perceived them as a wild and violent rogue religion that believed in multiple gods and that at points in its history practiced polygamy and violence against non-members (see the section on Mormon History and Beliefs, below).

For the last few decades, however, the Mormon church has made a concerted effort to improve its image and portray its members as pious, clean-living, family-oriented, and friendly toward Christian groups.

This has not resulted in a doctrinal change. Mormonism still holds that all other churches, including the Catholic Church, are products of the Great Apostasy and that they do not hold the true faith of Jesus Christ. They do not recognise the baptisms or other sacraments of Christian churches as valid, and they make organised efforts to convert Christians to Mormonism.

This is carried out through a variety of means, but notably by many young Mormon men, who are encouraged to spend a period of time doing missionary work. It is often through these missionaries that Catholics come into contact with Mormonism.

Mormon History and Beliefs

Who was Joseph Smith?

Joseph Smith Jr. was born in 1805 in the state of Vermont but spent much of his time growing up in New York state. He came from a religiously unorthodox family and, according to the Mormon church's official account, he experienced a spiritual awakening when he was fourteen years old. He claimed to have received a vision in 1820 of God the Father and Jesus Christ, who informed him that all existing churches were corrupt and that he should not join any of them. This experience - known as the First Vision - is pivotal to Mormonism and is often depicted in its art.

Subsequent to the First Vision, Smith claimed to be visited on several occasions by an angel named Moroni. This angel informed him that he would be given the task of translating writings on golden plates that were buried in a local hill, now known as Hill Cumorah. Smith claimed to have received possession of the plates and began to translate them in 1827.

The translation method was unusual, as was the language in which the inscriptions were allegedly written. According to Smith, the texts were composed in an unknown language he referred to as "Reformed Egyptian." Not knowing this language, Smith required supernatural assistance to translate it. According to some accounts, he used a pair of stones set in silver eyeglass frames, which he referred to as the "Urim and Thummim." Other accounts state that he used a "seer stone" that he put in his hat, into which he put his face. He then saw the translation in these stones and dictated it to various scribes.

At the end of the translation process, Smith returned the golden plates, so they are not available for inspection today. In fact, they were not available for inspection in his own day, either. They were reportedly shown only to two select groups of individuals. These individuals signed statements that are printed in the front of the Book of Mormon under the titled "The Testimony of the Three Witnesses" and "The Testimony of the Eight Witnesses."

The Book of Mormon was published in 1830, shortly before Smith founded the Mormon church. Originally he called it "the Church of Christ" (no relation to other churches of the same name), but he changed its name on several occasions - each time reportedly at the direction of God - until in 1838 he had settled on its present name.

The church also changed its headquarters frequently. Though founded in New York state, it moved to Ohio in 1831, then to Missouri in 1838, and to Illinois in 1839. These moves were motivated in part by conflicts between the Mormon and non-Mormon communities. Violence and vigilantism were common, and eventually a conflict broke out known as the Missouri Mormon War, which the Mormons lost, prompting a relocation to Illinois.

When it was first formed, the doctrine taught by the Mormon church was not that different from Protestant Christianity. Mormons claimed to have an extra book of Scripture focused on the history of Israelites and Jesus Christ in the Americas, but the major doctrinal distinctives for which they later became famous were still unknown. The Book of Mormon and other early Mormon works contain no references to the existence of multiple gods, to the ability of men to become gods, or to polygamy as a positive thing. Indeed, the Book of Mormon forcefully condemns polygamy (*Jacob* 2:24-28, 3:5) and forcefully asserts the existence of only one God (*Alma* 11:26-31) - sometimes stressing God's oneness to the point of making it appear that the Father, the Son, and the Holy Ghost are simply three modes of one Person rather than three Persons who are one Being (*Alma* 11:38-39, *Mosiah* 15:1-4).

How did Mormon doctrine begin to change?

In 1835 the foundations of two Mormon distinctives were laid. In this year Joseph Smith bought several Egyptian mummies and papyri from a travelling show. He also began to have sexual relations with a young woman named Fanny Alger, who was living in his household.

The purchase of the Egyptian papyri led to the Mormon teaching of polytheism, which Mormons often refer to as the existence of "plural gods." Smith announced that he could translate the papyri and, in 1842, Smith published the result. It is now known as the "Book of Abraham" and is contained in the Pearl of Great Price. The work purports to be a first-person narrative written by the biblical patriarch Abraham. It states that God's throne is near a star or planet named Kolob, which rotates every thousand years. It also introduces the doctrine of eternal intelligences and identifies at least some of these as gods who organised the heavens and the earth out of pre-existing matter.

Smith's relationship with Fanny Alger played a role in the development of his teaching of polygamy, which Mormons often refer to as "plural marriage." The Alger affair became known, which caused friction with Smith's wife, Emma, and with Oliver Cowdery, who was one of the "Three Witnesses" to the Book of Mormon plates and who held high office in the church.

Fanny Alger is often taken to be the first of Smith's "plural wives" (after Emma, his first wife), but we do not have documentary evidence that he was ever "sealed" to her. Documentary evidence does exist that he was married or sealed to numerous other women in his lifetime, and in 1843 Smith claimed to receive a revelation (now *Doctrine and Covenants 132*) in which polygamy was expressly authorised. This revelation also stated that men and women must be eternally sealed to each other in marriage or they cannot advance to godhood. It stated that the purpose of polygamy is to allow more souls to be born in human form. And it commanded Emma to accept the other wives that had been "given" to Joseph or she would be destroyed.

How did Joseph Smith die?

Joseph Smith was killed in a gun battle in Carthage, Illinois in 1844. At this time Smith was the mayor of the nearby town of Nauvoo, Illinois and was running for president of the United States, though his candidacy was not regarded as having a serious chance of success.

On 7th June, a group of disaffected Mormons in the town published a single edition of a newspaper - the Nauvoo Expositor - that was sharply critical of Smith, arguing that he had tried to marry their wives, that he held too much power, and that he had become a fallen prophet due to his introduction of false teachings, including polytheism and polygamy.

In response, Smith and the city council ordered the printing press destroyed. This provoked harsh criticism since freedom of the press is one of the basic guarantees of the U.S. Constitution. There was talk of bringing Smith up on legal charges. Fearing mob violence, Smith declared martial law in Nauvoo on 18th June and called for a local Mormon militia to defend the town.

A trial was proposed in the nearby town of Carthage, which was non-Mormon. Smith considered fleeing rather than submitting to arrest, but criticism from his followers dissuaded him. He surrendered to the Carthage authorities on 25th June on the charge of inciting riot and was quickly charged with treason against the state of Illinois for having declared martial law in Nauvoo. Other council members also surrendered and were charged with offenses, though some were released on bond.

On 27th June, a pistol was smuggled into the Carthage jail and given to Joseph Smith. Later that day a lynch mob approached the building and stormed the area where Smith and his companions were being held. Smith's brother, Hyrum, was shot in the face, and Smith fired his pistol at the mob, striking several individuals. He then attempted to leap from the jail's window when he was shot in the back.

Because Smith died in a battle with a lynch mob, he is often regarded by Mormons as a martyr. He would not be regarded as a martyr in Christian terms since, unlike Jesus and the Christian martyrs, he did not accept death for his faith but died while trying to flee his opponents after having been unsuccessful in killing or otherwise deterring them with a gun.

What happened after Smith's death?

A succession crisis ensued that led to the creation of several different Mormon offshoots. The largest group was led by Brigham Young.

A new conflict broke out, known as the Illinois Mormon War, following which Young relocated the community to what is now the state of Utah. This was not part of the United States at the time, and the territory was run as a theocracy by Brigham Young. Polygamy was widely and openly practiced. Tensions with the United States continued and were thrown into sharp relief in the Mountain Meadows Massacre, in which Mormon forces slaughtered a group of settlers from Arkansas who were making their way to California.

The Utah Mormon War of 1857-1858 left the United States in control of the Utah territory, but tensions continued. When the U.S. Congress outlawed polygamy, at first the Utah Mormon community refused to comply. Both the third and the fourth Mormon prophets - John Taylor and Wilford Woodruff - went on the lam from the law and spent years in hiding to avoid arrest and prosecution for defying the laws against polygamy. Eventually, though, the pressure became too great, and Woodruff issued a manifesto (now appended to *Doctrine and Covenants*) in which he disassociated himself and the Church from polygamy. He did not condemn it outright, but he indicated it would not be actively taught or encouraged. On another occasion he claimed to have received a vision from God showing him that the Mormon church would be ruined if polygamy continued to be preached.

The fifth Mormon prophet - Lorenzo Snow - gave the classic expression of the Mormon view of God and man by stating "As man is, God once was; as God is, man may become." He coined this couplet before he was president, but it became a famous summary of the core teaching of Mormonism.

In the 1950s the Utah church began an aggressive outreach program, which involved a standardised presentation of the Mormon message. The Church also encouraged all members to regard themselves as missionaries, not just the young men devoting full-time efforts to mission work.

Throughout the twentieth century, Mormons worked to rehabilitate the image of their church. They had been perceived by many as violent, polygamous polytheists. Now that Utah had achieved statehood, they sought to present themselves as loyal Americans, as opponents of Communism during the Cold War, and as clean-cut, family-oriented people who practiced monogamy. Many of the more unusual teachings advanced by previous Mormon leaders - such as Brigham Young's claim that God the Father had been Adam - were retired.

A particular sore spot in the latter half of the twentieth century was the Mormon church's stand on race. From the time of Joseph Smith onward, Mormon teaching had held that the colour of a person's skin was connected to his spiritual state. The Book of Mormon speaks of dark skin being given to people as punishment for their sins (2 *Nephi* 5:21), and it indicates that this curse can be lifted, resulting in white skin upon spiritual improvement (3 *Nephi* 2:15, 2 *Nephi* 30:6). Interracial sexual intercourse was considered gravely sinful (2 *Nephi* 5:23). Some Mormon leaders held that black people were born black because they had sinned as spirit children in their life before birth.

Mormon leaders had repeatedly issued statements affirming the inferiority of black people, and blacks were prohibited from the Mormon priesthood. But changing social conditions once again resulted in a change of Mormon doctrine. The U.S. Civil Rights Movement altered American race relations, and the Mormon church's exclusion of black people from the priesthood came increasingly to be seen as unacceptable and racist. Organised protests against this practice were conducted. At the same time, the Mormon church was planning to open a temple in Brazil, where many of the converts to Mormonism had some degree of African ancestry.

In response, Mormon prophet Spencer W. Kimball announced in 1978 that, following extended prayer and meditation, he had received a revelation that henceforth the priesthood should be open to people regardless of race or colour. He did not repudiate prior Mormon teaching regarding race, including the statements in the Book of Mormon regarding dark skin being a curse.

Given the changing nature of Mormon teaching, where may it go in the future?

This is something only time will tell. One Mormon offshoot group - the Community of Christ - has cast off so many of its original distinctives that it is now more like a theologically liberal Protestant church - except with extra scriptures and ceremonies.

How the Utah Mormon church will evolve in the future is not clear, but one possible direction was indicated by the fifteenth Mormon prophet, Gordon B. Hinckley, in an interview he gave in 1997 to the San Francisco Chronicle, in which the following exchange occurred:

Q: There are some significant differences in your beliefs. For instance, don't Mormons believe that God was once a man?

A: I wouldn't say that. There was a little couplet coined, "As man is, God once was. As God is, man may become." Now that's more of a couplet than anything else. That gets into some pretty deep theology that we don't know very much about.

Q: So you're saying the church is still struggling to understand this?

A: Well, as God is, man may become. We believe in eternal progression. Very strongly [*Musings of the Main Mormon*, 13th April, 1997].

This exchange sent shockwaves through the Mormon community. The prophet not only appeared dismissive of former prophet Lorenzo Snow's celebrated summary of the main doctrine of Mormon theology, he also appeared to waffle on the question of whether God used to be a man.

Non-Mormon observers took this as an indicator that current Mormon leadership may be willing to allow the church's theology to develop in a direction more congenial to Christian teaching. Whether this is so remains to be seen. In the meantime, Mormonism must be evaluated in terms of its present official teaching.

A Catholic Critique of Mormonism

How would a Catholic evaluate Mormonism?

The first step in evaluating Mormonism is to recognise the difference between Mormonism as a system of belief and the character of individual Mormons. As with any group, there are individual Mormons who are good and bad. Many Mormons are ordinary, sincere individuals who are trying to follow God's will as they understand it. While this is a credit to them, it does not mean that their beliefs about God are correct.

It is also crucial to recognise that Mormonism as a system of belief is not Christian. This is especially important because most non-Christian religions do not attempt to portray themselves as Christian. Hindus or Shintoists may believe in multiple gods, but they don't claim to be the true followers of Jesus Christ. The fact that Mormonism tries to present itself as Christianity - and, indeed, as the true Christianity - while rejecting the most fundamental doctrines of the Christian faith can lead to enormous confusion if its non-Christian status is not kept clearly in mind.

What reasons would one give for preferring Christianity to Mormonism?

In the most basic terms, Christianity is simply more credible than Mormonism.

Christian apologists have for centuries produced positive reasons for believing in the Christian faith. These include philosophical proofs of the existence of God (as a single, supreme Creator who is infinite and who possesses all perfections, as opposed to a finite being who is constantly growing and changing and who is only one of a multitude of such beings).

The case for Christianity also includes proofs of the resurrection of Jesus Christ, which shows not just that monotheism is true but that Jesus Christ in particular is a true prophet whose teachings can be trusted, including the fact that he is the Son of God.

There are also numerous avenues by which the historical reliability of the Christian Scriptures can be demonstrated. While not everything in the Bible is intended by the authors to be taken literally, when the authors make historical assertions, these are true, and the historicity of the Bible is supported by archaeology, paleography, and the historical sciences.

Evidence of this nature can be found in many works of Christian apologetics, but a particular work surveying many of these lines of evidence is the *Handbook of Christian Apologetics* by Peter Kreeft and Ronald K. Tacelli, SJ.

How do the arguments for Mormonism compare to those in favour of Christianity?

They do not fare well. Mormon apologists have not produced a comparable body of literature providing sound arguments for polytheism. Joseph Smith had no miracles comparable to the resurrection of Christ to attest to his reliability as a prophet, and he has a record of making failed predictions. Finally, the Mormon Scriptures lack credibility.

Though they may propose arguments on some issues - particularly when responding to objections to their faith - Mormon missionaries generally do not seek to demonstrate the truth of Mormonism by providing objective reasons to believe that it is true. Instead, they invite potential converts to pray about whether the Book of Mormon and its claims are true, with the promise - from a passage in the Book of Mormon (*Moroni* 10:4) - that if they do this then God will reveal to them that the Book of Mormon is true. The missionaries will bear witness that they themselves have done this and have had such a confirming experience, which is commonly described as a "burning in the bosom."

What is an example of a failed prediction by Joseph Smith?

In 1832 the state of South Carolina was involved in an event known as the Nullification Crisis, in which it threatened to nullify federal law and there was much talk of it seceding from the Union.

That same year, Smith prophesied: "Verily, thus saith the Lord concerning the wars that will shortly come to pass, beginning at the rebellion of South Carolina, which will eventually terminate in the death and misery of many souls; And the time will come that war will be poured out upon all nations, beginning at this place. For behold, the Southern States shall be divided against the Northern States, and the Southern States will call on other nations, even the nation of Great Britain, as it is called, and they shall also call upon other nations, in order to defend themselves against other nations; and then war shall be poured out upon all nations" (*Doctrine and Covenants* 87:1-3).

Needless to say, neither the Nullification Crisis of 1832 nor the U.S. Civil War (1861-1865) resulted in a world war. The First World War did not break out until the 20th century and it was not brought about as European states became involved in strife between American states.

This prophecy is part of the official Mormon scriptures today, and it is manifestly spoken in the name of the Lord ("thus saith the Lord"), which means that the biblical test of a true prophet applies: "When a prophet speaks in the name of the LORD, if the word does not come to pass or come true, that is a word which the LORD has not spoken; the prophet has spoken it presumptuously, you need not be afraid of him" (*Dt* 18:22).

Why do the Mormon Scriptures lack credibility?

One reason is Joseph Smith's claims regarding how the Book of Mormon was produced. According to Smith, an angel led him to golden plates in the Hill Cumorah on which the original texts of the Book of Mormon were written in "Reformed Egyptian." He then was miraculously enabled to translate these plates before they were returned.

This means that the plates are not available for inspection. Nor did Smith make them available for ordinary inspection in his own day. Various individuals reported being shown an object wrapped in a table cloth or a pillow case or enclosed in a box, and Smith told them this object was the golden plates, but the people were not allowed to see the object for themselves.

The Book of Mormon contains two notices - known as "The Testimony of the Three Witnesses" and "The Testimony of the Eight Witnesses" - which state that the individuals named as witnesses saw the plates. However, statements made by some of the witnesses later indicated that they had only seen the plates in a vision or that they had only handled an object that was concealed from their sight.

One early Mormon, Martin Harris, served as one of Smith's scribes in writing the Book of Mormon and also provided funds for its production. Harris's wife, however, did not believe Smith's claims regarding the work and to convince her Smith allowed Harris to take 116 pages of the manuscript to show her. These pages were then lost and Smith did not simply re-translate them from the plates. Instead, he produced an abridgement of the material, which he claimed was found in "the small plates of Nephi."

On another occasion, Martin Harris demanded to see the golden plates and Smith said that he could not himself show them to him but that he would go into the woods to the place where they were and that if Harris followed Smith's tracks in the snow, he would find them. Harris followed these instructions but did not find them.

These incidents undermine the credibility of the Book of Mormon. Its credibility is further undermined when read against Smith's background as a former "money digger" - an occupation in which he used the same "seer stone" he used translating the Book of Mormon to unsuccessfully search for valuable minerals or buried treasure.

Consider the situation: Someone with a background as an unsuccessful psychic treasure hunter claims that he has been given a set of golden plates. Yet he consistently refuses to show the plates to individuals and only allows them to see an object hidden in a covering. He leaves a trail in the snow to where the plates are, yet when this trail is followed the plates are not discovered. When part of the translation of the plates is lost, he does not simply re-translate it. To attest to its authenticity he publishes statements from witnesses who later say that they only saw the plates in a vision or that they handled a concealed object. And once the translation is done he has to return the plates so nobody can see them again.

This set of facts is much more consistent with the hypothesis that Joseph Smith was a confidence trickster and that the plates never existed than with the hypothesis that he was a prophet of God in possession of real golden plates.

Are there other problems with the credibility of the Book of Mormon?

A notable problem is that there is an absence of historical and archaeological confirmation for the book. This is particularly striking when compared to the historical and archaeological support that exists for the Bible.

The Bible was written in three languages (Hebrew, Aramaic, and Greek) that are known to have existed because we have evidence for them in the form of ancient inscriptions and manuscripts, and dialects of them are still spoken today. These languages can be translated and understood by many.

The texts in the Bible refer to numerous places that either still exist (Jerusalem, for example) or whose remains have been discovered by archaeology (Capernaum, for example). They refer to ancient peoples who still exist (Egyptians, Chaldeans, Samaritans) and to civilisations whose archaeological remains have been excavated (Hittites, Philistines, Moabites).

The Bible records individuals known from secular writings to have existed, such as Alexander the Great, Cyrus the Persian, Herod the Great, Herod Agrippa, Pontius Pilate, the Emperors Augustus, Tiberius, and Claudius, among others.

Nothing like this is the case with the Book of Mormon. There is no historical evidence that "Reformed Egyptian" existed. We have no ancient inscriptions or manuscripts written in this language. No one can translate it. It is not mentioned in historical writings.

With the exception of Hill Cumorah, no sites mentioned in the Book of Mormon can be identified today, and some Mormon apologists even question whether Joseph Smith's Hill Cumorah is the same one mentioned in the Book of Mormon due to problems with the geography described in the book. None of the civilisations the book mentions have been discovered by archaeologists. None of the people it mentions can be shown from other sources to have existed.

There is simply no historical or archaeological evidence that the language, the cities, the civilisations, or the people of the Book of Mormon were anything other than the product of Joseph Smith's imagination.

Are there credibility problems
with the other Mormon Scriptures?

There are. We have already noted that the work known as Doctrine and Covenants contains failed predictions of Smith's, such as the prophecy that the Nullification Crisis would lead to a world war.

A particularly striking example of a credibility problem concerns a work known as the Book of Abraham. Smith claimed to have translated this from papyri purchased from a travelling mummy show in 1835. He also published a set of facsimile images taken from these papyri and his commentary on the various elements in the facsimiles.

Ancient Egyptian was not a commonly known language in Smith's day and the hieroglyphic system of writing was deciphered by a contemporary of Smith - the French scholar Francois Champollion. But today this language is well understood, and it is clear that Smith's interpretations of the pictures and hieroglyphics in the facsimiles are simply wrong. For example, what Smith identified as a depiction of the sacrifice of Isaac is, in reality, a funeral rite being performed for a dead Egyptian man named Hor, and what Smith identified as a scene of Abraham seated on a throne is in fact a depiction of the Egyptian god Osiris judging the dead.

In addition to the facsimiles, portions of the papyri Smith used in translating the Book of Abraham also exist. None of them mention Abraham, and none of them correspond to the text of the Book of Abraham.

What is to be made of the "burning in the bosom" to which Mormon missionaries appeal?

This cannot be considered a reliable indicator of the truth of a religion. People's imaginations can lead them astray.

The fact that the Book of Mormon promises that God will reveal its truth to those who ask him proves nothing. The verse that supports this idea (*Moroni* 10:4) is an attempt to get people into a receptive frame of mind in which they will be guided by their feelings rather than by objective evidence. If people are in that state of mind, a certain number of them are guaranteed to experience a positive feeling toward the Book of Mormon - either because they are excited by the idea of a new and previously unknown volume of scripture or because they like the wholesome, family image that Mormons project or because they want to have the same religion as their family or friends.

None of this proves the truth of a religion. Feelings come and go, and they are not to be depended upon - particularly when objective evidence is at hand, and the objective evidence regarding the Book of Mormon and the other Mormon scriptures indicates that they cannot be trusted.

In addition to Moroni 10:4, Mormons also appeal to James 1:5 as a basis for praying about the truth of the Book of Mormon. This verse states: "If any of you lacks wisdom, let him ask God, who gives to all men generously and without reproaching, and it will be given him." This verse contains an affirmation that God will give wisdom to those who seek it from him, but it does not promise that God will give every person a private revelation about whether a particular work is a book of scripture.

First, there is no promise of private revelation at all. One might pray for wisdom and then be guided by God to objective evidence to help one make a decision. There is no promise here that God will give one subjective feelings in response to the request for wisdom.

Second, wisdom is most naturally understood as guidance about what practical decisions one should make (e.g., "Would this course of action be sinful?" "Should I get married?" "Should I enter religious life?"). This is not the same thing as determining whether a book is Scripture.

Thirdly, what we have said about subjective feelings still applies. In seeking wisdom from God, one should rely on the objective evidence he provides since feelings are not reliable. Putting subjective feelings over objective evidence is not wise, and Christians should not pray about the truth of the Book of Mormon because to do so disregards the objective evidence that God has provided and opens oneself up to the subjective world of feelings.

What is one to make of Mormon claims concerning the "Great Apostasy"?

The Mormon view of the "Great Apostasy" is very problematic and, in fact, counts as evidence against Mormonism.

Scripture reveals that toward the end of the world there will be an apostasy or falling away from the Christian faith (2 *Th* 2:3, 1 *Tm* 4:1), however Mormons have radically reinterpreted this as an event occurring not at the end of time but early in Church history.

This is necessary in order to explain the existence of the Mormon church: If God already had a Church on earth then there would be no need for him to start a new one. Consequently, Mormons claim that the early Church apostatized - fell away from the true teachings of Christ - and a new church had to be started through Joseph Smith.

This apostasy also had to occur very early on, because if one reads the writings of the early Church Fathers, one does not find them endorsing Mormon theology. While some individual writers among the Fathers may have had unique views on one point or another, in no case does one find them teaching a Mormon worldview. Their theology is unmistakably Christian, meaning that the Great Apostasy - if it occurred - had to occur exceptionally early.

But there are problems: Why is there no record of the Great Apostasy? We know about numerous heresies that were combated in the early Church because the Church Fathers mention and condemn them in their writings. They describe the views of their opponents in order to refute them. If the Church Fathers were a bunch of apostates who fell away from an original Mormon faith then why don't they talk about people with a Mormon worldview as being among their opponents?

An apostasy is going to cause theological controversy, and there should be literature produced as part of that controversy as the parties argue back and forth. Even after the controversy is over there will be a memory of it, just as historians today know about the heresies that arose in different periods of Church history.

Indeed, when Mormonism arose in the 19th century, one of the first things that happened was the development of a body of controversial literature in which Mormons and Christians critiqued each others' positions. If the same thing had happened in the early Church - with Christianity breaking away from Mormonism rather than the reverse - then the same thing would have happened, but it didn't.

This is a historical reason to disbelieve the Mormon view of the Great Apostasy, but there are also biblical and theological reasons to disbelieve it. First, the Scripture passages that speak of the apostasy refer to it occurring "in later times" (1 *Tm* 4:1) in connection with "the coming of our Lord Jesus Christ" (2 *Th* 2:1) and the appearance of the antichrist (2 *Th.* 2:3-4).

What is more, Jesus Christ himself indicated that his Church would survive, telling the apostle Peter, "You are Peter, and on this rock I will build my church, and the powers of death shall not prevail against it" (*Mt* 16:18). He also assured his followers: "Lo, I am with you always, to the close of the age" (*Mt* 28:20).

If one takes Jesus at his word, if one has faith in him and his word, then there is no room in God's plan for the Church Christ established to apostatise and have to be re-started by someone else.

What is one to make of the Mormon view of God and man?

This is another exceptionally problematic Mormon belief. In fact, it is the single most important reason why Mormon theology is not Christian, because it involves a denial of the central teaching of the Christian faith, which is its understanding of God.

Mormonism holds that there are a multitude of gods and that man and God belong to the same species, so that men can become gods in the same sense that the Father is God.

These claims are expressly rejected in Scripture. The Bible makes it abundantly clear that there is only one

God. Its treatment of this matter is stark. In Isaiah 44:6, the Lord flatly states: "I am the first and I am the last; besides me there is no god." A chapter later he declares: "I am the LORD, and there is no other, besides me there is no God... There is none besides me; I am the LORD, and there is no other" (*Is* 44:5-6).

There were never any beings before the Lord who were gods, nor can new gods come into existence. Thus God declares: "Before me no god was formed, nor shall there be any after me" (*Is* 43:10).

This is not to say that by divine grace men cannot come to resemble Christ, sharing in his holiness and thus "become partakers of the divine nature" as St Peter puts it (2 *P* 1:4; cf. *CCC* 460), but it is to say that man cannot become so godly that he can cross the line into full fledged divinity of the sort that God possesses.

Dealing with Mormons

What should one do if Mormon missionaries appear at the door?

It depends on a number of factors. The first and most important factor is your knowledge of and security in the faith. If you know the Christian faith thoroughly and are firm in your commitment to it then you may choose to perform a spiritual work of mercy for the missionaries by sharing the Christian message with them.

On the other hand, if you are not well educated in the faith or if you are plagued by doubts then it would be better not to talk with them.

Or you simply may not have time to have a discussion or be prepared to receive visitors.

Whatever the case, you are under no obligation, and you can politely say that you aren't in a position to speak with them and close the door.

If you do choose to talk with them, it is important that you do so with great charity. It is very easy - particularly given some of the facts of Mormon history and problems with the Mormon scriptures - to sound as if one is mocking their faith. People do not respond well when they think you are mocking what they hold sacred. You wouldn't respond well, either, if your most cherished beliefs were mocked, so follow Jesus' dictum: "Do unto others as you would have them do unto you" (*Mt* 7:12).

One must be honest with them about the problems with Mormonism, the reasons why it is incompatible with Christianity, and the truth of the Christian faith, but one must do this in a manner that is gentle and kind so that one is "speaking the truth in love" to use St. Paul's phrase (*Ep* 4:15).

Mormon missionaries often wish to continue the discussion beyond a single session. If you choose to allow them to come back, use the time between meetings to learn more about Mormonism. There is much to know, and the better prepared you are, the better you can serve the missionaries by planting seeds in their minds that may one day lead them to the Christian faith. See the resource recommendations at the end of this booklet for ways to learn more about Mormonism.

How should one relate to Mormon acquaintances or relatives?

The same way one should relate to other non-Christian acquaintances and relatives. One should treat them with respect and charity, pray for them, and at opportune times try to share the Christian message with them.

The last will pose special challenges in the case of Mormons because they already view themselves as

Christians - in fact, they view themselves as the adherents of the true teachings of Christ. The realisation that this is not the case will come, if it comes, only in stages. Consequently, you should never expect anyone to convert in front of you. What you want to do is plant seeds that may sprout later.

You also want to plant seeds in the most productive way. This means not mocking their beliefs; it means not allowing discussions to turn into arguments; and it means not allowing discussions to get sidetracked with minor matters.

For example, Mormons perform proxy baptisms for the dead and appeal to a verse in 1 Corinthians to support the practice (1 *Co* 15:29). The meaning of this passage is not clear. It can be translated and understood several different ways (see Inside Mormonism by Isaiah Bennett for a discussion of these). But the question of whether baptisms can be performed by proxy is a very minor matter that one should not spend a lot of time on.

The question of how baptism may or may not be performed pales in comparison to the importance of issues like whether there is one or more than one God, whether men can become gods, whether Christ can be taken at his word when he said that his Church would survive, and whether there are better reasons to believe in the Christian Scriptures than the Mormon scriptures.

Can Christians work together with Mormons in social and political matters?

In the United States Mormons have been very active politically and Christians have found ways of working together with them on a variety of subjects. Mormons have a broadly pro-life and pro-family ethic, which has made it possible for the two groups to work together on life issues such as abortion and family issues including greater parental authority concerning the education of children and opposition to homosexual "marriages".

While Mormonism tends to be broadly pro-life and pro-family this does not mean that their views will always coincide with the teachings of the Church. For example, Mormons may be willing to allow abortion in some cases and some Mormons (particularly those in splinter groups) may not recognise marriage as an exclusive union of one man and one woman.

Despite these differences, it is often possible for Christians and Mormons to work together in the social and political spheres, though this must be done in a way that does not create confusion about the fact that Mormonism is incompatible with Christianity.

How can one share the gospel with Mormons?

The core of the gospel is the fact that God has sent his Son, Jesus Christ, into the world, that he has made it possible for us to be saved through his death and resurrection, and that God now summons all men to become part of his Son's Church and await his return.

Mormons will acknowledge all of this. The problem is that they interpret it in a radically different way. Sharing the gospel with Mormons thus means helping them understand the true meaning of the gospel, which will cause the discussion to centre on facts such as these:

- There is only one God.

- The Father, the Son, and the Holy Spirit are three Persons who are one Being, not three separate deities.

- Jesus died and rose again so that we might be forgiven our sins, share life with him in heaven, and become godly but not so that we would become gods in the sense that he is God.

- Christ meant what he said when he proclaimed that the powers of death would not prevail against his Church. This means that the Church he founded in the first century did not apostatise but it is still here with us today in the form of the Catholic Church.

As you explore these points, expect Mormons to come back with arguments and Bible passages to support their position. For example, when the fact that there is only one God is discussed, Mormons often appeal to 1 Corinthians 8:5-6, in which Paul says that "there are many 'gods' and many 'lords' - yet for us there is one God." But when this passage is read in context, it is clear that the "gods" and "lords" Paul is referring to are pagan divinities such as those worshipped by the Greeks and Romans. He is saying that many people worship a variety of gods, but we Christians recognise that there is only one God, for just prior to this passage he proclaimed that "we know that an idol has no real existence, and that there is no God but one" (1 Co 8:4).

The correct interpretation of passages that Mormons appeal to can often be spotted by simply reading the passage in context and against the conflict with paganism that early Jews and Christians found themselves in. There is also an extensive Christian literature responding to Mormon interpretations of Bible passages, so if how a passage should be taken is not immediately obvious, simply consult the many resources that are available on the subject, either online or in print.

In discussing the gospel with Mormons, pay particular attention to their views of the origin and destiny of man and ask commonsense questions. For example, concerning their belief that our souls existed before this life, ask why we can't remember our prior life if that's the case. If they respond that God caused us to forget as part of a test or to help us learn better, ask how having less knowledge rather than more would help us succeed or learn. No earthly father, if he had the power, would cause his children to forget things that they already learned in order to test them or help them learn more. This does not appear to make sense.

Similarly, in discussing the destiny of man, encourage Mormons to think about this matter concretely. Do they really believe - in their heart of hearts - that one day they could be the god of their own planet, with billions of people worshipping them? Do they really want that - and why? Do they really think it's possible or do their hearts tell them that there is something wrong with this goal?

Share your own faith with Mormons in an upbeat and positive way as a contrast. Talk about what it means to you to be not a biological child of a finite god but a creature who the infinite Creator of the universe has lovingly adopted into his family. Talk about the sense of relief and gratitude you have when your sins are forgiven and how you look forward to being with and worshipping the source of infinite goodness for all eternity, not being worshipped by others as you rule over some planet.

As always, be respectful and gentle as you do this and portray Christianity as a positive and attractive alternative to Mormonism, both in terms of its view of man and God and in terms of the evidence that exists to support it.

What other resources are there for dealing with Mormons?

There are a wide variety of them. A good place for online resources dealing with Mormonism is the website of Catholic Answers (*www.catholic.com*), which contains numerous articles on the subject. There are also many print and audio resources that can be found through this web site and others.

Unfortunately, not all books on Mormonism are of consistent quality. Good ones include *Inside Mormonism* and *When Mormons Call* by Isaiah Bennett. These books discuss Mormonism from a Catholic perspective.

Also good is the book *The New Mormon Challenge*, which was edited by Francis Beckwith, Carl Mosser, and Paul Owen. Although written for an Evangelical Protestant audience, this book has important information that can benefit the Catholic reader. *The Changing World of Mormonism* by Jerald and Sandra Tanner, though somewhat dated, is also a valuable Protestant treatment of Mormonism.

Informative Catholic Reading

We hope that you have enjoyed reading this booklet.

If you would like to find out more about CTS booklets - we'll send you our free information pack and catalogue.

Please send us your details:

Name ....

Address ....

....

....

Postcode...

Telephone...

Email ....

Send to: CTS, 40-46 Harleyford Road,
             Vauxhall, London
             SE11 5AY

Tel: 020 7640 0042
Fax: 020 7640 0046
Email: info@cts-online.org.uk

 **CTS**